PROPHET OF MY
OWN LIFE

to

Hal & Rebecca

God Almighty will
reward your Kindness!

Sergio A

SERGIO ALVARADO

Unless otherwise noted, all scripture is from the *King James Version* of the Bible.

Scripture quotations marked *New Living Translation* are from the *New Living Translation* © 1996, 2004, 2007, 2013 by Tyndale House Foundation. Used by permission of Tyndale House Publishers Inc., Carol Stream, Ill. 60188. All rights reserved.

Prophet of My Own Life

© 2019 by Sergio Alvarado
PO Box 1548 I Springtown, TX 76082 I prophetofmyownlife@gmail.com

ISBN 978-1-7331004-0-3

24 23 22 21 20 19   6 5 4 3 2 1

Editorial by Jordan Media Services I P.O. Box 761593 I Fort Worth, Texas USA
www.jordanmediaservices.com

Cover Design by Brian Duffield

Book design by Chris Eberhardt

Praise for *Prophet of My Own Life*

I have been blessed to know Sergio Alvarado for the past 15 years. Every time I am with him, everything he touches becomes more like Christ. Reading this book will establish in your heart the power of the Living God. You will see the journey of one individual who had no hope of being alive, let alone being an asset to society, be transformed and become a powerhouse for God. Full of the grace of God, this book will strengthen, encourage and thrust your life forward.

Bill Krause
Family Community Church
North Highlands, CA

Sergio Alvarado is a man with a heart for people to know the redeeming and restorative power of the gospel of Jesus Christ. I have witnessed this man in action, doing the work of the Lord. I've been in his home, and with him in ministry. He is the real deal! This book will bless you!

Pastor David Leggett
New life fellowship
Council Bluffs, Iowa

In our prayer time we always pray that God brings to us divine connections and friendships — those that will be a blessing to us and to whom we can bless and grow together in the Lord.

We are so grateful that God has brought Brother Sergio Alvarado into our lives as part of those divine connections. We are blessed to call him our friend and family. His humbleness and testimony have been a blessing and an inspiration to our lives, and we know that it will be the same to every person who reads this book and hears his testimony (Jeremiah 29:11).

Pastors Ignacio and Nuvia Hughes
Ministerios Palabra de Fe
Douglas, Ariz.

Walking and finding your God-ordained purpose is crucial to living a fulfilling and purposeful life. By unlocking his own life's journey, Sergio Alvarado shows us how to find our own path and reveals how your journey can shape your future. My friend Sergio is a brilliant speaker and mentor. His love for seeing people journey through life with an overcoming spirit will leave a lasting impact in your life. Prophet of My Own Life shares his personal experiences and revelations, from the highs and lows of life. They will resonate with you, prove valuable and provide applicable wisdom to your own spiritual life. This book will be a road map to lead people closer to God.

Wilfredo Santos, Founder/Senior Pastor
Destined for Greatness Faith Center
Saginaw, Texas

I met Brother Sergio when he and I were paired together to count inventory in an old, freezing warehouse at Kenneth Copeland Ministries. Though two people could hardly be any more different, the Lord quickly knit our hearts together like that of David and Jonathan. Though my upbringing was world's different than his, and though I can scarcely imagine the hardships he has faced, Sergio's testimony of God's inescapable love and His ability to turn around even the worst of circumstances continues to astound me whenever I see him preaching to the people. I'm honored and privileged that God has partnered me with this man, and am excited to see what God has in store for him next!

Chris Eberhardt
Chris Eberhardt Ministries
Haslet, TX

Dedication

I dedicate this book first to GOD, and to His son JESUS! To my wife, Yvette who has been with me through the good times and the not so good times. To my children, Sergio Jr., Eric, Leslie, Andy and Albert. To my friend Barry Tubbs, a man I look up to and who has been a great example and strong inspiration in my life. And to my mother, Roberta Arredondo, and my father, Sergio Alvarado. In my heart I know they loved me and did their best by me and my siblings.

Contents

Foreword

I have known Sergio Alvarado, and his wife Yvette, since 2005 when they first came to Kenneth Copeland Ministries. We have had the opportunity to work together on several ministry projects and meetings, both domestic and international. These were my best observations of Sergio's character, determination and integrity.

I have witnessed a pilgrimage that has resulted in him becoming who he is and where he is today. No doubt, he has surprised many who were skeptical of him early on. But then, no one should be surprised at what God can do with and through any individual who will submit to His leadership and authority in simple faith and obedience. I praise God for the ministry He has entrusted to Sergio and Yvette, and I am grateful that He used me in some way to contribute to the foundation of their ministry.

Any person who follows the basic truths in this book, and applies them in their daily life, will be a stronger, more mature disciple. Furthermore, they will enjoy a closer communion with Jesus.

A minister's heart and soul are greatly demonstrated through his speaking and writing ministry. If a minister is compassionate and full of the grace of God, it is evident. If he has a real-world experience of ministering the love of God to people, it will be reflected in his ministry to all. This is certainly the case with my close friend Sergio Alvarado, and it is very obvious in his new book, Prophet of My Own Life. I know Sergio Alvarado well. I've watched him grow through the things that it takes to be a true disciple of Jesus. Follow him as he follows Jesus through every page of this book. Your life on the victory side is there for you. Take it! Don't every let it go.

Barry E. Tubbs
Senior Associate Minister
Kenneth Copeland Ministries

Introduction

I wrote this book with the intention of encouraging people who have gone, or are going through hardships. Whether you are addicted to drugs, come from a broken home, have suffered abuse, endured divorce, are dealing with low self-worth, or anything else, I am convinced that you are responsible for the outcome of your life. Every day—every second, minute, and hour—there is the opportunity to change the things that are holding you back, if you want to change them. If you don't like who you have become, or where you are in life, then you can make a solid decision to change it. Perhaps you've tried to change and have not seen any results. Don't give up! I was there—with no hope! I made many mistakes. But one day I made the decision to change, and I reached out to God. And gradually, my life began to change—for the good. It's not easy, but it is possible.

I don't know where you are in life, but what I do know is that God can meet you there. And He can help you change. Through His Son, Jesus, He has made the way for us to escape the evil traps of the devil. If you will just reach out to Him, by faith He will touch and help you. He will change your life. There is hope. Be strong. Be courageous. Trust God, and never give up. It's not how you start, it's how you finish!

Sergio Alvarado

Chapter 1

Hope for a Hurting World

The phone ringing shortly after midnight was more a distraction to me than anything. After spending the past three days getting high on cocaine, and the last couple of hours in a bar drinking to calm me down, the last thing I needed was to be talking on the phone—especially late at night.

Sleep was best. Hours and hours of sleep.

My head still throbbed from the alcohol, but I forced myself off the sofa and reached for the phone.

Mr. Alvarado, your father just passed.

"Mr. Alvarado," the voice on the other end said, "this is Thomason General. You asked us to call you if there was any change in your father's condition. Mr. Alvarado, your father just passed, and we need you to come back to the hospital."

Though I'd been strung out on drugs for the past three days, those words rang clear.

My dad had died.

I had just talked with him hours earlier. I had gone to the hospital to see him. Until that time, it had been at least seven years since we had last seen or talked to each other. It was also one of only about a dozen times that I had seen my father since I was 2 years old. That's when he walked out on my mother, my younger brother and me.

"Thanks," I said in the most concerned voice I could muster. "I'll come down."

My father was an alcoholic. I don't know for sure, but he may have also used drugs. What I do know is that because of his heavy drinking, an early death was almost certain for him. That night, in a hospital in El Paso, Texas, alcohol stole his life when his liver shut down.

I'd like to say my dad's death had a major impact on me, that losing him rocked my world. I wish I could say I was devastated because I'd just lost my best friend. After all, that's what dads are supposed to be, right? Our best friends in the entire world.

I wish I could say I cried. Uncontrollably even.

But none of those things happened.

Though I hurt for my father, and his sudden death saddened me, hearing that he had died only reminded me of an even worse tragedy in my life that had occurred two years earlier when my mother died.

But her death was no surprise either.

At age 50, after spending most of her life hooked on drugs and alcohol, and working as a prostitute, she had dropped dead on the street in my native town of Juárez, Mexico.

I was 18 when she died.

If anything shook me the night my dad died, it was that fact that the deaths of both my parents had caused me to think about my life. I questioned what I had become as a result of how I had seen them live their lives. I had started drinking when I was about 12 years old. By the time I turned 16, I was experimenting with marijuana and other drugs.

Standing next to my dad's still body that night in the hospital, chills ran down my spine. Suddenly, reality was staring me in the face. Sobering thoughts penetrated my confused mind.

Is this how life for me is going to end? I wondered.

Have the experiences of the last 19 years prepared me for nothing more than a coffin? Am I staring my future in the face?

Everyone has a story.

Here, on these pages, is where I tell mine. Not so people can feel sorry for me, but rather to bring attention to the conditions that still exist, and the young people being affected by them—not just in Juárez, Mexico, where I was born, but around the world.

It's time we stand up and fight, especially for our young people.

Over the years, the culture and lifestyle in the city of Juárez has not changed. "Heroin Alley," the place where people from the United States flood across the border to score heroin, still exists. People still mill around in the streets, some cooking drugs in spoons or snorting cocaine out in the open while 12-year-old boys peddle drugs to earn money to help feed their families. The narrow streets are still lined with bars and brothels, and beautiful young girls, some as young as 15 and 16, who prostitute themselves.

I tell my story hoping it will bring awareness and create hope.

That's what the children living in Juárez need. They need to be shown the way out—the way to escape.

My 20-plus year addiction to drugs and alcohol didn't disappear overnight. Neither was it easy for me to discover the path of freedom. Both were tough battles. But I'm pleased to say each was won through my persistence and a hard-and-fast decision that what I needed was a serious relationship with God—something that had begun for me when I became "born again" at age 7, but soon after walked away from. My aunt would take my mom, my younger brother, Horatio, and me to a little Pentecostal church in Juárez. It was there that, though I didn't understand what it meant to be "born again," I was touched, marked for God. For the first time in my poor, misguided life, I heard about God and I loved what I heard. It gave me hope!

> I realized that to be free, my spirit had to be free.

Reflecting on the deaths of both my parents, and where I was in life, I realized that to be free, my spirit had to be free. I needed a connection with God,

That connection came through my escape from drugs.

It came when, later in life, I heard a pastor in El Paso, Texas, say one day that "God is on your side." No one had ever told me that before. Not in my family, not among my friends. No one. Hearing those words gave me something I had only experienced as a 7-year-old child in a small church in Juárez: a sense of hope!

And it also came when a preacher named Kenneth Copeland caught my attention as I heard him say, "You are the prophet of your own life." Those words grabbed me like nothing has ever grabbed me since. I hold on to them to this day, realizing that I don't need drugs or alcohol to live. I don't need a crutch to lean on or identify me or dictate how far or where I will go in life. I only need God.

I truly am the prophet of my own life!

I once heard a story about two brothers: They grew up in the same family, but their characteristics were totally opposite.

Someone once asked one of the brothers, "Why are you an alcoholic?" He told them, "Because I grew up in an environment of alcoholism."

Then, they asked the second brother, "How come you don't drink?"

"Because I grew up in an environment of alcoholism," he responded.

The Bible says in Deuteronomy 30:19, "I call heaven and earth to record this day against you, that I have set before you life and death, blessing and cursing: therefore choose life, that both thou and thy seed may live." In the New Living Translation that verse reads like this: "Today I have given you the choice between life and death, between blessings and curses. Now I call on heaven and earth to witness the choice you make. Oh, that you would choose life, so that you and your descendants might live!"

> In life we have choices. We get to choose.

As a child growing up in such horrendous conditions, it never occurred to me that I had something to do with how my life played out. But the truth is, in life we have choices. We get to choose. Our circumstances don't have to dictate where we go or what we want to be or do. Growing up, I didn't understand that. I thought what my environment dictated was what I was supposed to be, and that's what I gave in to. Today, I realize just how wrong that is. I also understand how deadly it can be.

Through my work as a minister, I often have people ask me why I did drugs. I don't know that my answer satisfies them, but it's the only one I have.

It was my choice. It was a bad one, but it was the one I made.

Using drugs and abusing alcohol are choices. The good news is, stopping is also a choice. By no means am I suggesting that it is easy. It's not. But with God's help, anyone can be freed from drugs, alcohol and any other addiction.

Recently, I returned to Juárez—not just as a former citizen but as a minister of the gospel. I carried a heavy burden on my heart for the people, but especially the children. I stood inside the basketball stadium where, as a child, I sold potato chips at the concession stand. And I visited the place nearby where my mother worked at the bar. At the Lord's direction, I had rented the stadium and was there to host the first ever Juárez Victory Campaign, a Christian event that included pastors from Lima, Peru, Venezuela and across the United States. Instead of attending a sporting event, that weekend people had come to the stadium to praise the Name of Jesus.

Juárez is still considered one of the most dangerous cities on earth. That, I believe, is why God has called me to go back there: to help make a difference, particularly among the children. Under His direction, we are planning to purchase land in the area where I once lived and am now developing plans to construct a facility where children can come to hear the Word of faith preached. It will include a kitchen and dining area so they can also be fed and nourished.

God has called me to take the message of hope to a hurting, dying world—to throw out a lifeline to the children of Juárez.

Chapter 2

Life In 'Heroin Alley'

In 2010, a media outlet called the GlobalPost released an in-depth report titled "The Seven Circles of Juárez." The subtitle read: "The murder capital of the world and those who dwell in its unique hell." The report offered startling, and most disturbing statistics regarding the drug culture that then existed in the city of Ciudad Juárez, Mexico—the place I was born. Here's some of what the report had to say:

If Dante had ever been to Juárez he would have placed it squarely in the seventh circle of hell, the one housing 'violence' and 'ringed' by a river of boiling blood. The city, which lies on the Rio Grande just across from El Paso, Texas, is the murder capital of the world, claiming more than 5,500 killings since January 2008. It is responsible for one-fifth of the more than 25,000 drug-related murders that have occurred in Mexico since 2006 when President Felipe

Calderon officially declared war on the country's heavily armed drug cartels.

That national war reached another dramatic turning point last month when the front-running candidate for governor in a drug-torn Mexican border state was assassinated by gunmen believed to have been sent by a drug cartel. Nowhere is the violence more horrific than in Juárez, where 13 teenagers were murdered at a party and 17 recovering drug addicts killed at a rehab center. But amid all the media spotlight on this butchery, the facts of who exactly is fighting, who is dying and why remain misty and confusing to many observers...

Most sources, including the FBI and various non-governmental organizations, find that it is. In 2009, Juárez had 191 homicides for every 100,000 inhabitants, according to Mexico's Citizen Council for Public Security. In second place was San Pedro Sula, Honduras, with 119 killings. New Orleans, America's most murderous city, had a rate of 69 killings, putting it in eighth place. The United States as a whole has an annual murder of about 5 per 100,000. Of course, many homicides both in Juárez and around the world are never reported.

That was in 2010.

In June 2018, in an online article where the headline read, "Murders in Mexico Border City of Juárez Continue to Rise As Deaths Top 160 in June Alone," the El Paso (Texas) Times reported that "in all of 2017, there were 767 homicides in Juárez... By comparison, there were 19 murders in El Paso in all of 2017."

The article described the present atmosphere in Juárez:

> There have been more than 160 homicides during a blistering June, compared with about 120 deaths a month ago... U.S. and Mexican law enforcement officials have said that the violence is due to fighting among drug-dealing groups, drug cartels and a conflict between ... crime organizations. The violence has been raging in Juárez for months despite increased patrols by state, federal and local police. The number of monthly deaths have more than doubled from earlier this year. According to the city's Mesa de Seguridad y Justicia, or security and justice board, there were 65 homicides in April, 56 in March, 43 in February and 72 in January.

While some may find it hard to fathom that such staggering figures as these are true, or that living conditions so deplorable and appalling anywhere on the face of the earth truly exist, nothing could be further from the truth. The sad reality is that this was, and continues to be the culture in Juárez, Mexico.

I was born into that culture in 1962—the fifth of six children.

My mother, Bertha Arredondo, had lived in the U.S. before my birth. That's where three of my four siblings were born.

My mother had her first child at age 12.

Most of what I know about my mother is first hand. I lived it. But there's so much I don't know, and so much more I sometimes wish I didn't know. For instance, I know that my mother had her first child at age 12, after her parents gave her up to some strange man who happened by and took an interest in her. From what I'm told, my grandparents were dirt poor and couldn't properly provide for her, so they told the man to just "take her."

He was 26.

By the time she was 21, my mother had given birth to three more children, two boys and one girl. She never married the man, but the two lived together. At some point, before she gave birth to me, they moved to Juárez, where I'm told that several years later he left my mother, who he abused, and took up with a younger woman who he verbally and physically abused.

From that time on, life was difficult for my mom. Now on her own, my mother had no means to provide for our family. After she met my dad, and I was born, and then my younger brother, things got even worse.

Although she was uneducated, my mother had some great qualities, most notably her beauty. Unfortunately, she learned quickly how to put that quality to work in order to survive. Because she was uneducated and had no working skills, she had a hard time finding work. Eventually, she went to work at a local bar.

That's when the drinking began.

Soon, she turned to prostitution.

They both quickly became a lifestyle for her.

Inside 'Heroin Alley'

I was 2 when my dad walked out on us. By then, my four older siblings had also gone off in different directions. Two of my brothers had started using heroin, and my sister was married to a drug user.

We lived in an area called "Heroin Alley." Hundreds of people routinely crossed the Mexican border almost daily from the U.S. to buy heroin in Heroin Alley. The entire area was, and still is to this day, drug infested—littered with bars and brothels, and crawling with prostitutes. On any day, people could be seen sitting in public—smoking dope, shooting up with needles and syringes, or cooking crack cocaine in spoons over open flames. As a child growing up in Juárez, this is what I saw every day.

By the time I was 6, I understood what poverty was. I also realized that we were steeped in it. We moved around a lot because my mother had problems paying the rent. One of the houses we lived in had no roof, no cement floors and no windows. When it rained, we got soaked. We got heat from kerosene lanterns and the cooking stove. There was also no refrigerator.

Sometimes, my mother would leave home and be gone for several days. Even then, I knew she was not working the bars but was with men. Sometimes she brought men back to our little three-room, one-bedroom house and entertained them there.

To say my relationship with my mother was good wouldn't be true. It was more a love-hate relationship. I loved her when she was not drinking or doing drugs. Those were some of the most memorable times for Horatio and me. She was a different person when she wasn't drunk. Sometimes, she would love on us and sing to us. Other times, we would all climb in bed together, my brother on one side and me on the other, with my mother sandwiched in-between. We just enjoyed the warmth of her body next to ours.

But more often, we saw the other side of her: the side that saw her so drunk or strung out on drugs that she hardly knew us or where she was. At times she would turn violent, screaming and yelling obscenities, mainly at me. She would curse, and I would curse back. Once, I was so angry that I yelled and told her, "I hope you die!" She screamed back at me: "You're not my son!"

I was angry a lot. And scared.

Angry because we never really had our mom to ourselves. And scared because I was afraid that someday we would lose her—either to alcohol, to drugs, or worse. Fear became my constant companion as, every day, I worried over my mother. It got so bad that, at one point, I was always expecting someone to come up to me and tell me that my mother was dead.

That fear almost became reality one day when my mom suddenly passed out while at home. She and three male friends were sitting at the kitchen table, drinking, when she started having convulsions and fell to the floor. I was 7 when it happened.

Frightened, I ran to her side. But no sooner had I dropped to my knees, than one of the men shoved me aside and yelled at me, "Get away!"

By looking at her, they recognized she had overdosed on heroin.

From a corner in the room, I watched, embarrassed, as two of them stripped my mom's clothes off, carried her to the shower, and turned cold water on her. When they removed her top, I could see small blood dots on her arm—dots I recognized as needle marks. While the two showered her with cold water, the other man mixed a solution of water and salt, put it in a syringe, and injected it into my mother's arm. Moments later, she came to.

Incidents like that were not common, at least not when she was around us. But because my mother was always high, the likelihood of something like that happening was always a possibility.

Aside from the drugs, my mom suffered from grand mal seizures. I have very vivid memories of times when those seizures happened. She would convulse, and her body would jerk around with such force that it was hard to control her. Her friends had told me to wrap a spoon with tape and always keep it handy. When my mother did have a seizure, I was to put the spoon in her mouth to prevent her from biting her tongue. I would also turn her face-up as she lay on the floor and put my feet under her head to keep her from striking her head against the floor or anything else while she was jerking.

Sometimes, when the seizure ended, she would lay on the floor and sleep for as long as an hour. When she became conscious, I would wrap a towel tightly around her head to relieve the pain from the massive headaches that were sure to follow. I'd stay by her side the entire time, and when she was well enough to get up, I would clean her up as best I could, wiping the spit and foam from around her mouth while making sure she was OK.

On a number of occasions following these episodes, my mom sent me to the nearby liquor store. She said the alcohol helped to ward off the pain, but even at such a young age I knew she wasn't being truthful. I understood she was just feeding her addiction. The owner of the liquor store knew my mom and was used to me coming into his store. He never refused to sell me alcohol, even though I was underage. I would always enter the store through a back door so people wouldn't see me. The owner would stuff the bottle of liquor down my pants and then send me back out the same way I came into the store.

Just Let Me Die!

Times like these were exhausting.

I sometimes thought, No child should have to live like this.

I wished for a normal life. But living in Juárez, and in the conditions that surrounded us, normal wasn't easy to define. More than anything, it was what you choose to make it. Not every child faced the kinds of things I experienced. In fact, only about 20 percent of the children growing up there faced similar situations as mine.

There were times I just wanted to die.

Despite my young age, I can recall feeling old. I wanted out of the kind of life I had been forced into, but I didn't ever see that happening. There were times I just wanted to die.

At one point, one of my aunts, my mom's sister offered to take Horatio and me in and care for us, even though she had several kids and was living in poverty. Though I wanted to go live with her, I refused to leave my mom. Despite all her faults, I loved her and I felt it was my responsibility to take care of her.

By the time I was 9, my mom's drinking and drug use had gotten worse. She couldn't keep a job, which pushed her further into prostitution. We never lived in the same place more than a year. In fact, I'm pretty sure the entire time we lived in Juárez we stayed in no fewer than 20 different houses.

My mom was regularly arrested for public drunkenness. Most of the time, I had to get money from relatives to bail her out of jail.

My one escape from the reality of what was happening to and around me was school. School saved me because, if just for only a few hours each day, I wasn't afraid. I didn't worry, and I didn't always have an upset stomach. School was my temporary escape. It was like entering another universe; an alternate reality. But even that turned out to not be fail safe.

I loved basketball, and I enjoyed going to my school's games. To make money, I sometimes sold potato chips at the concession stand at the school's basketball stadium. My mom also sold drinks at a bar right next to the concession stand. Sometimes, as I listened to the roar and cheers coming from the crowds in the stadium, I pictured my mom with one of suitors. In my mind, I could hear the embarrassing sounds I used to hear when she was entertaining one of her "customers" in the room (sometimes the same room) next to where I was trying to sleep.

Chapter 3

A Little Taste of Heaven

I remember the first time I heard about God.

When I was 7, my aunt took my mother, Horatio and me with her to a little Pentecostal church in Juárez.

I can still remember my first reaction upon entering the building.

It was nothing like how most churches look today.

There were no stained-glass windows, and no towering steeple on top. There was no fancy glass chandelier suspended from a vaulted ceiling, and a band did not accompany the singing. There was only an old, upright piano.

Inside this small, rustic adobe the benches were old and scarred, and the cement floors cracked. There was no praise team, nor any skilled musicians. Yet, in this place there was light. A kind of light that shone so brightly it seemed to overshadow all darkness. Despite all the destruction and hopelessness that filled the city, and the pervasive atmosphere of drugs, alcohol and death that surrounded them, the congregation was happy. They sang, they danced, and they gave praise to God. I could feel the excitement. And I loved it. I loved hearing the minister preach and tell stories about Jesus. I loved it so much so that, although I didn't know what it meant to be born again, I gave my life to Christ.

> I loved hearing the minister preach about Jesus.

Being in church also changed my mom. She stopped drinking and using drugs. As best I could tell, she also stopped messing around with men.

Apparently, my aunt had told the pastor about my mom, and that she had been on drugs and was working the streets. He owned a small, one-room house near the church and allowed us to stay there rent-free. In return, we cleaned the church. That only lasted about a year, however, because my mom eventually started drinking again and everything fell apart. For example, one day I came home from school and opened the door only to find my mother and two of her friends sitting at a table with opened bottles of liquor. I literally exploded with anger. So much so, that I screamed and cursed at them, and knocked over the table. I just couldn't understand why my mom kept going back to this way of life. In that single moment, my world came crashing down. I cried all day long.

It became worse from there.

By the time we moved from Juárez to Fort Worth, Texas, in the United States, my mom's drinking had spiraled out of control.

Church as My Refuge

We spent nearly a year going to church with my aunt. During that time, I experienced good things I will never forget.

There's a story in the Bible that describes how some parents once brought their children to Jesus, hoping that He would pray for them. When the disciples learned the children were there to see Jesus, they scolded the parents for bothering Him. Jesus corrected His disciples, telling them: "Let the children come to me. Don't stop them! For the Kingdom of Heaven belongs to those who are like these children" (Matthew 19:14, New Living Translation).

It would be years before I would know what the "Kingdom of Heaven" was all about. But for the short time I spent going to church with my aunt, I got a little taste of heaven.

I will always be grateful for my aunt, who thought it good that, at a young age, I be introduced to Jesus. Not only had she planted a seed in my heart that gave me hope, but little did I know that experience would later change my life forever.

After my mom went back to her old lifestyle, we stopped going to church.

The experience of seeing my mom become sober, only to return to her old lifestyle, had for some reason soured me against church. It also turned me against God. I thought my mother's fall was my fault. I thought God was mad at me, so I became mad at Him.

Cycle of Poverty and Despair

In 1972, when I was 10, we were living in one of the worst sections of Juárez with an uncle, his wife and three children. We slept on the floor, but considering all we had already been through, we were just thankful to have a roof over our heads.

My uncle, an alcoholic, was very abusive to his family, which made living with them very uncomfortable. After being there a couple of months, one of my older brothers came to Juárez, packed up all our belongings, and moved my mom, Horatio and me to Fort Worth, Texas, illegally. At that point, we had become homeless. Instead of solving our problems, the move complicated matters. We spoke no English, and the fear I had known every day of my life threatened to overtake me as my mother spiraled deeper into uncontrollable darkness. One might think living in the United States was a good thing, that we had finally escaped the hardship of Juárez. But that wasn't the case.

The only thing different was the location.

We still had no money, and the house where we lived was infested with crawling and flying cockroaches—hundreds of them! There was no electricity, no running water, and the restrooms were located on the outside. We slept on the floor. The living conditions didn't concern me so much because I had experienced much worse while living in Juárez. What did worry me, though, was the fact that we were considered aliens and that we could be arrested and eventually separated. My brother, who was a full-blown addict, helped us to get settled, but he didn't stick

> The fear I had known every day of my life threatened to overtake me...

around. So, we couldn't rely on him for financial help.

The poverty we endured wasn't just limited to our living quarters. I well remember the times we had very little to eat, or had no food at all. The owner of one of the places we lived had a dove feeder that stood about 12 feet above the ground. My mother would have me go with her to the feeder in the middle of night. I carried a bucket with me, and would turn on the water faucet on the premise that I was getting water. The truth, though, was that we used the sound of the running water as a decoy so that my mom could steal doves from the feeder for us to eat. The noise from the running water would also frighten the doves while they were sleeping. When the doves stirred, my mom would snatch a couple of them, break their necks to kill them, then carry them back to the house where she would make dove soup for us to eat.

To help keep a roof over our heads, Horatio and I delivered newspapers and washed dishes. Meanwhile, my mother, just like before, often left home and was gone for days at a time. When she didn't come home, I'd go looking for her. Often, I would find her passed out on a bench in the neighborhood park. If that didn't cause enough embarrassment, some of my friends knew about my mom's indiscretions and would often tease me when I went to school.

I remember one night she stayed out, and I waited up for her. I thought she might have one of her men friends with her, so I prepared myself.

In the stillness of the night, I sat upright in my chair after hearing a noise. I watched through the window as my mother staggered toward the door. A man followed close behind. Holding a knife in my hand, I heard myself say these words: "Try to bring a man in this house and I'll stab him!"

My mom knew I was serious. A similar incident had happened when we lived in Juárez. I stabbed that man in the leg. After she came inside alone, I took up my place as sentinel at the door. The man turned around and left.

Later, as she slept, I tossed a rope across her and tied her to the bed to keep her from getting up and leaving again. Before leaving, I looked down at my mom as she slept and said, "Are you ever going to stop? What's it going to take?"

As the years passed, I enrolled in school and learned English. I also made friends and got acclimated to my new surroundings.

Abandoned and Rejected

I was 16 when my mom pulled another one of her disappearing acts. By now, I was more than used to her being gone, but this time she hadn't come home for four days. Afraid of what I might discover, I set out to find her—scouring park benches, and every bar and brothel I knew of in Fort Worth. Worry and fear gripped me as I wondered what could have happened to her. Bad thoughts whirled through my mind: Has she gone on a binge with a dangerous man? Is she dead? Might she be lying in a hospital somewhere? Maybe she's been arrested.

These were the fearful thoughts and emotions that had plagued me as a youngster in Juárez.

I also wondered what would happen to Horatio and me if my mom didn't return. How would we survive alone in a foreign country?

Finally, we heard from someone that my mom had been seen back in Mexico. She had returned to Juárez—without Horatio and me. In effect, she had abandoned us. With our mom now gone, there was no way Horatio and I could survive on our own. Even though we were both now working part time, we didn't make enough money to keep a roof over our heads. Plus, we were illegal aliens.

"We've got to get back to Mexico!" I told Horatio.

We pooled our money and bought a little car for $400. Although neither of us knew how to drive, we figured it couldn't be that hard. Laying a map across the scarred kitchen table, we mapped out our journey, packed what few belongings we had, and headed for Juárez. After stopping in El Paso, where we stayed a few days with our sister, I was back in Juárez. This time, I was on my own because Horatio stayed behind in El Paso.

Within a couple of weeks, I located our mother. By this time, she was living on the street again. At that point, through sheer desperation, she was drinking anything that contained alcohol, including cologne. For days, she was filthy, having not taken a bath. Sometimes, her face would be bloodied and stained from striking it against the pavement when she fell because she was drunk or because of the seizures. Her lips would be busted, swollen and torn, with some of her front teeth either knocked out or broken because of her constant falling.

For a short while after finding my mom, she and I went to live with our sister. My aunt's husband had passed and she had room enough so that we could stay with her. That didn't last long, however, as our mother's addictions led her right back to the streets.

When I returned to Juárez, I had been determined to find my mom and help her to get her life in order. I knew I needed money to do that, so I quickly found a job working with some of my family members in the fields. Every morning at 2 o'clock, we boarded a bus in downtown El Paso and rode to one of several fields in New Mexico where, from sun-up to sun-down, we picked cotton, onions, cucumbers or peppers. It was hard work, but I managed to save my money and use it to buy some land. Eventually, I had enough money to start building a small, two-room house for my mom and me to live in. Unfortunately, my mom never got to live there.

One day, I was sitting at a bar when one of my cousins walked in, came up and sat down next to me. I could tell by the look on his face he was about to tell me something I didn't want to hear.

"I just saw your mother," he said.

Instantly, something cold coursed through my veins.

"Was she dead?"

"Yeah."

"Where was she?"

"In the street."

For a brief moment, I sat still—crying, but at the same time feeling an awful confusing mixture of sorrow and relief. In a flash, thoughts of the past, and all Horatio and I had endured with my mom and her addictions, swirled through my mind. Then, remorse set in. I felt like I'd spent my whole life trying to keep her alive, and I had failed.

My mom was only in her early 50s when she died—alone in the street—the victim of alcoholism.

I drank the rest of the night—almost non-stop.

Losing my mom was a turning point in my life. I'd experimented with drugs while living in Fort Worth, but after her death I was consumed with despair, confusion and hopelessness. I knew I was following in her footsteps, but now I felt powerless to stop. I was headed into an abyss of drugs and alcohol that would last the next 20 years.

Chapter 4

A Vicious Cycle

To say my dad was an absentee father would be too generous. My dad left us when I was 2 and moved to El Paso. I saw him less than a dozen times in my entire life after that.

One of those times was the night he died.

I remember that night as well as I remember my mom's death.

It began the way most everything in my life began back then. Me, alone in my apartment and stoned out of my mind on cocaine. I had moved to El Paso after my mother's death.

A friend called to tell me he had heard there was a man at the local hospital with the same name as mine. He was very sick, and hospital authorities were trying to locate his nearest relatives. Although my dad came from a good family, one that had money, his problems with alcohol had estranged him from them. Not that they had disowned him, but apparently he chose to not associate much with them. I was told he had been living on the streets.

Even though I hated my dad for what he had done to our family, for some reason I felt obligated to at least go to the hospital. Maybe, deep down inside, I wanted to see my dad again.

I recognized him as soon as I walked into the room.

He recognized me, too.

At first, it was small talk. Then, the conversation turned to my mom.

"How's your mom doing?" my dad asked.

"Dad, she passed away two years ago," I told him.

For a moment, there was silence. The same kind of silence that filled the bar the night my cousin told me my mom was dead.

Suddenly, there were tears streaming down his face.

Seeing my dad cry was something I'll never forget.

"How did she die?"

"In the streets."

"Sergio, I'm so sorry."

I don't know why my dad ever left us, or what happened between him and my mom to make him walk away. But at that moment, I sensed a degree of sincerity in those words. I felt he was truly sorry he had abandoned us.

"There's nothing to be sorry about," I encouraged him.

Then I heard myself say, "I forgive you."

By that time, we were both crying.

After my mother died, I had fallen headlong into drugs—not just using them, but also selling them. I had a little money, and I lived in a nice apartment.

I heard myself say, "I forgive you."

"When you get out of here, you can come live with me," I told my dad. "You're going to be fine," I assured him.

Suddenly, I felt no malice toward my dad. All the hatred I had kept bottled up inside me for those many years was gone—vanished! All that mattered was that I wanted to see my dad get better. I didn't want to see what happened to my mom happen to him. Unfortunately, that didn't happen.

I left the hospital that night confident that my dad would be fine. Once he got out of the hospital,

I reasoned, he would come to live with me. At 22, I suppose I hoped we could somehow restore the years we'd lost through separation. I remember saying to the nurse, "Whatever he needs, you call me."

I'm ashamed to admit it, but even then I was high on drugs. Yet, I meant those words. I really had sympathy for my dad, and I wanted a relationship with him.

After leaving the hospital, I walked the four blocks along Alameda Street—headed straight to a bar. I needed something to help bring me down from the drug high I was on. I stayed there for about an hour, then went back to my apartment. That was when the phone call came telling me my dad had died.

Horatio was with me when we went to the hospital.

The nurse who met us remembered my visit from just a few hours earlier.

"He should have been dead days ago," she told Horatio and me, "because his liver was completely destroyed. He was just waiting for you guys."

Rejection Runs Deeper

I recall once when my father took Horatio and me to meet his family in El Paso. I'd never met my grandmother, but she was a very sophisticated-looking woman and somewhat on the wealthy side.

My grandparents lived in a big house on the good side of town, furnished with lots of nice things. I still have memories of the few times we visited there. I was always fascinated by the two large, bay windows that adorned the front of the house, and the large, glass front door.

Although we carried the family name, and my dad had named me after himself, his family was never very receptive toward my mom, Horatio and me. They didn't like us and looked down on us—mainly because of my mom and what she had become. On one of our visits, I remember my grandmother becoming very abusive toward Horatio and me. Sitting at the dinner table, she openly criticized and belittled our mom, saying all kinds of ugly things. Things like, "Your mom's a prostitute!" and, "You're not my grandchildren!"

The more she talked down about my mom in disgust, the angrier I got.

When I couldn't take it any longer, I got up from the table and walked outside. Out of anger and rejection, I picked up the largest rocks I could find and began throwing them at the house. The rocks shattered some windows on the front of my grandparent's house.

The hatred toward my brother and me reached further than just my grandmother.

When we went to my dad's funeral, other family members made their feelings known as well. I had wanted to serve as a pallbearer at the funeral, but knowing there was strong animosity, I suspected that my wishes would be met with opposition from the family. I was right. Not only did they snub their noses at my request, the family asked us to leave the funeral altogether. I didn't get to be a pallbearer, but we stubbornly stayed for our father's funeral.

Like Mother, Like Son

From the time my mother died, my drug use worsened. I realized I was following in her footsteps and that, just like her, I was powerless to stop. I also realized the only difference between my mom and me was in appearance. Though I was falling apart on the inside, I gave the outside appearance that all was well. I overdosed on cocaine several times.

After my dad died, things got worse for me. I spent the next several years of my life chasing drugs. Many times, when I would use cocaine, I would wake up only to find myself covered in blood from nose bleeds. I had snorted so much cocaine that my nose had cuts on the inside. I recall once, after I'd been using cocaine for about 16 hours straight, I stumbled outside a bar into the bitter cold. I couldn't find my car keys so I could drive home, so I jumped into the bed of my friend's truck and almost immediately fell asleep. When I woke up, I was inside my friend's apartment. I went to the restroom and looked in the mirror. My face was covered with blood.

By the time I was 37, I was a full-blown cocaine addict. I not only took drugs but sold them to help support my habit. Most everyone I knew was doing drugs. I spent most of my time going back and forth between Juárez and El Paso. If I wasn't dealing drugs, I was working a legitimate job, so I always had a place to live.

By the time I was 37, I was a full-blown cocaine addict.

I can recall a time, when I was about 10 years old, that my brother used me as a decoy while he stole money from some drug addicts who had come to him to buy drugs. It was one of the most frightening times in my life.

As I remember it, my brother had assured a group of about five men, that he knew where he could buy some drugs, and had told the men to give him the money and wait while he went to purchase the drugs. It was very common for people to be ripped off when trying to buy drugs, so the men were suspicious of my brother from the beginning. When they asked for an assurance that he would come back with their drugs, my brother told the men he would leave me with them as a guarantee.

Unbeknownst to them, my brother had already discussed with me his plan to steal the men's money and told me how to escape from them.

"Wait five minutes after I'm gone," he said, "then take off running as fast as you can."

I recall that the men had me sit down between two of them, so they could keep an eye on me. Scared to the core, I sat quietly as my brother left to go buy the drugs.

Though the men were already high on drugs, they watched me intently.

When five minutes was up, I took off running as fast as I could, scared for my life that if they caught up to me they would hurt or kill me. Two of the men came after me, running as fast as they could. For a short while they were close behind me, but soon they stopped running, probably because the drugs caused them to tire easily, and I escaped.

I ran to our house, which was about 10 blocks away. When I arrived at the house, I was crying uncontrollably. Still afraid that I would be caught and killed, the first thing I did was go to the bathroom where I began to vomit. Vomiting had become almost a normal thing for me as a child because I lived in constant fear—mainly that something would happen to my mom.

Later, I saw my brother. Still nervous, afraid and angry, I began cursing at him. We got into a big argument over what had happened, and despite what I went through, he never apologized. Instead, he told me to "grow up and be a man." To this day, I don't truly understand how he, being 10 years older than I was, didn't realize how I could have been so afraid and angry over what had happened. Maybe the drugs had more of a grip on his mind than I knew at the time. I just know that at that moment, I wanted to punch him out.

That wasn't the only time my brother and I were partners in crime. Once, when I was 9, he and I were arrested inside a store for shoplifting.

It was Christmastime, and my mother's boyfriend had taken my brother and me shopping under the deception of buying us Christmas presents. Once inside the clothing store, he led us to a rack where he instructed us each to try on a jacket. When we found the ones we liked, we were to put them on, then leave the store. He said he would stay in the store and pay for the jackets.

I wish I could say I didn't know his plan was for us to steal the jackets, but I can't. I'd seen it happen before.

Honestly, I don't believe I really cared that we were breaking the law.

My brother and I did as we were instructed, and when we got outside we were stopped by a security guard. He took us back into the store, then called the police who came and took us to the police station. We knew we were in trouble, but we still we refused to give the police the name of our mom's boyfriend. After a couple of hours, they let us go. I remember telling my mom what had happened after walking the several miles to get home. I also remember that her response was very nonchalant, as though she didn't even care.

The department store incident wasn't the last time I would have a brush with the law. There were several more to come.

When I was 21, for instance, I was arrested in Juárez along with some friends after police stopped the car we were riding in for running a red light. I was driving. Not only had we all been drinking heavily and using drugs, but I had some drugs in the trunk of the car. When the officers noticed I had been drinking and told me to step out of the car, I tried to bribe them, which I quickly realized wasn't very smart. Then they asked me to open the trunk. When I refused, and they attempted to arrest me, a fight broke out between the officers, my friends and me. Eventually, reinforcements showed up, and we were all arrested and taken to jail.

Up to that point, despite all my dealings with drugs and alcohol, I had never seen the inside of a jail cell. It wasn't a pretty sight. At the police station, we were placed in a cell so overcrowded with other prisoners we could hardly move. Sleeping was always a challenge. At night some of us had no choice but to sleep standing up, while others sat on the floor with their feet sticking through the bars of the cell. Officers walking the floors on patrol would kick our feet and legs and order us to pull them back inside the cell.

Nearly every day at least one fight broke out inside the cell.

I don't recall how long my friends remained incarcerated, but after five days I was taken from the cell and told I was being transferred to Federal Prison. After being placed in a patrol car and driven to a desert area just outside of Juárez, the officers let me out of the car and said I was free to go. I later learned that a friend had paid for me to be released.

You would think that experience was enough to cause me to rethink the way I was living and make the decision to change. But that wouldn't be the case. Instead, my drinking and drug use just got worse.

Several years later, I was arrested twice in El Paso: once for driving under the influence and another time for public intoxication.

Looking back over that period in my life, I can't help but think that something was stirred inside me back when I visited church with my aunt. God started doing something in me then, and He was still doing it—even though I was living in rebellion.

> God was doing something in me then, and He was still doing it.

The funny thing is, while I was destroying my life by using drugs and abusing alcohol, I always had a sense that God was in my life. I could sometimes sense His presence. Though I was tempted many times, there were some things that I just refused to do. I can say the same from some people I hung out with—friends who went to church with me as a child. For most of them, however, they would eventually give in to the temptation. Some of them ended up in jail; others died.

I got married when I was 20 and had two children, a son and a daughter. I had also fathered a son through another relationship. As a result of my drug usage, I had done tremendous harm to the mothers of my children, and to my children. Unlike my father, I had made it a point to stay involved in the lives of my children as much as I could. To this day, there remains a strained relationship between one of my sons and me that I hope and pray will someday be resolved.

Up to that point, my life had become like a runaway train. My kids were the only thing that kept me alive. That became so clear one day when I arrived to pick them up for a weekend visit. I had spent the earlier part of the day drinking and getting high with a friend. One of my sons looked at me in disgust and asked, "Are you ever going to stop drinking? I don't want to be around you anymore."

The pain of hearing those words coming from one of my children was staggering. I had sunk so low that now my son didn't want to be around me. The thoughts of having to tie my mom to the bed after another of her drunken episodes and drug-addict spells to prevent her from seriously injuring or killing herself, came rushing back.

That cycle was repeating itself—through me!

Chapter 5

A Cry for Help

I once heard someone say, "You are a product of your environment." At first, I didn't understand what that meant. But considering the kind of environment I was born into, it sounded like something I could surely relate to. In time, I figured it out—oddly enough through something I read in the Bible.

In 1 Corinthians 15, the Apostle Paul wrote in a letter to the Church at Corinth in which he said, "Be not deceived: evil communications corrupt good manners" (verse 33). Paul was warning the Christians at Corinth about false teachers who had come into the church teaching that the resurrection of Jesus Christ wasn't true. As a result of that false teaching, Paul wrote, the moral outlook on life they had was having a negative influence on some Corinthian believers.

From reading that scripture, I very quickly saw myself. I saw how the drug and alcohol addictions that had plagued my mom and dad all their lives had been passed on to me. I had picked up the habits of those who had surrounded me since early childhood—not because I wanted to but because I had been involuntarily exposed. The culture that existed in Ciudad Juárez, including the infestation of drugs, had infiltrated and destroyed the lives of so many people—including my mom. Now, it had laid claim on me. Being born in and spending my early years in Ciudad Juárez had guaranteed my life was going nowhere. I was doomed. Like so many of the kids still living in that region, I had been set up for failure and destruction.

Literally, I had become a product of my own environment.

All my life, I had watched my mother battle her demons. All my life I had done everything I knew to save her—to rescue her from the path of self-destruction she was walking on. But I had failed. I felt that I had let her, my brother and myself down.

I am convinced that deep down my mom wanted to stop drinking, to stop taking drugs and prostituting herself. The truth is, it wasn't that she didn't know how, or even how to get help. Many times, people had reached out to help her—especially the pastor and others when we spent that brief time in church. But nothing worked. She knew the harm her drinking was causing, and she was shown the way to escape. I believe that, in her heart, she wanted to be set free. She just didn't want it enough. She chose to not accept help. The influence drugs and alcohol had on her was so much more than she could handle. It was much stronger than her ability to say no.

My dad was different, because his environment was different. While he lived for a while in Ciudad Juárez, he made his home in El Paso, away from the influence of the drug culture that had overtaken hundreds of thousands of people. He came from a family that steered clear of drugs.

But drinking was a different matter altogether.

My dad had started drinking when he was young. And in the end, alcohol got the best of him. It dominated and eventually claimed his life.

Now that both my parents were dead, I was on a fast track to ending up just like them. Problem was, even though I hated it, I wasn't honest enough with myself to admit it.

Then, I saw a ray of hope.

A Black Moment and Turnaround

By the time I was 37, I was back in El Paso, still on drugs and living in a run-down trailer. One morning, after another night of partying and drugs, I awakened to a very windy, dusty day. Stepping outside my trailer,

I sat down in a folding chair and glanced up toward the heavens. I remember thinking how weary I was with life, how I so desperately wanted to be free from the curse of drugs. But I didn't know how to get free.

It had been a long time since I'd even thought about God, much less since I'd talked to Him. But for some reason, that morning I was honest with myself and realized I needed Him in my life. I wanted to talk to Him the same way I remember seeing my aunt talk to Him back in that little church in Juárez.

> God, if there's a chance for me to change my life, will You help me?

Suddenly, I heard myself say, "God, if there's a chance for me to change my life, will You help me? I'm so tired. Please help me."

I won't pretend anything supernatural happened.

I didn't hear a thunder clap, and I didn't see the lightning flash. I only know that when I uttered those few sincere words, a sudden peace came over me. I felt that God had actually heard my cry, and that He was going to help me. That day, I made up my mind that I was finished with drugs. Done!

Three days later, a friend stopped by my trailer and invited me to a bar.

Remembering I had made a fresh commitment to God, I refused to go.

A short while later, my nephew came by with the same invitation. At first I said no, but with a little coaxing, I decided to go.

They say God works in mysterious ways, and that He is always present.

I'm convinced that He does, and that He is.

Leaning against the wall inside the club, I watched as a beautiful young woman, whose name I later learned was Yvette, walked into the room. After getting up the nerve to approach her, I struck up a conversation. I asked her to go out with me. We had dated only twice before Yvette recognized that I had problems. She knew I was an alcoholic.

"Sergio," she said, "if you want to have a relationship with me, you have to change."

In time, I learned that Yvette had been married and divorced. She had been attending a Catholic church on occasion but stopped going to church after the marriage ended. Not long before she and I met, Yvette had determined to get her life back on track. She had seen a sign advertising an upcoming couple's enrichment class and was interested in attending.

Because we both had come from broken homes and had personal baggage, if anything was to come of our relationship she wanted it to start off right. So, she asked me to attend the class with her and I agreed. Unbeknownst to either of us, the class was held in a Christian church.

The first time we attended the class together, I was still hung over from drinking the night before. Yvette knew it, but she didn't let that stop us from attending the class. Instead of chiding me, she insisted we go.

That day, I rededicated my life to God. It was also the day I made up my mind that I was going to get free from drugs. This time, for real!

I began weaning myself off drugs in February 2002. During that time, I was also trying to restore my relationship with my children. I had already asked their forgiveness, and they had forgiven me.

However, my addiction didn't disappear overnight.

Many nights, for about six to eight months, I lay in bed suffering withdrawals, every cell in my body screaming out for relief. The withdrawals were so bad that I sometimes shook terribly. I also suffered severe headaches. I didn't tie myself to my bed like I had done to my mother. Instead, I would wrap myself in a huge blanket like a burrito and declare out loud, "I'm not moving!"

I sometimes wondered if this was how it felt for my mom those times when, by herself, she tried to kick the habit. I felt sorry for her. Sorry that she didn't have the strength to fight. Sorry that she didn't have anyone to stand with her and help her to get through it. At least I had Yvette, who not only insisted I go to church, but went with me.

> I realized that to be free, my spirit had to grow stronger in the Word.

It was a real struggle to get off cocaine, but going to church helped me to make it through. I realized that to be free, my spirit had to grow stronger in the Word of God, and I had to resist the devil. If I saw drugs on TV, my whole body shook. Certain sights and smells triggered the cravings. But finally, I was free. Free from drugs, free from the past and free to live a good life!

God Had a Plan

On May 31, 2002, three months after attending

that first class together, Yvette and I were married. Three years later, one of my sons and my daughter moved to Fort Worth. Hungry to rebuild a relationship with them, I decided to return to Fort Worth where I could be closer to them. The move meant I would be leaving another of my sons behind in El Paso, which was very difficult for me. I'd purposed to always stay as close to each of my children as I possibly could. But in my heart, I knew moving to Fort Worth was the right decision.

Getting settled, and finding work, wasn't easy. My brother and sister-in-law opened up their home to us while we looked for work. What money we had managed to save while living in El Paso was running out. At one point, things got so bad that we applied for food stamps. Though I felt in my heart that God had directed us to leave El Paso and move to Fort Worth, I couldn't help but wonder if we had made a mistake.

Then, one day my sister-in-law's sister was visiting when she overheard us talking about needing to find work. She said she worked at Kenneth Copeland Ministries and that there was an opening in the ministry's customer service department for someone who spoke Spanish. Neither of us was familiar with the ministry, but Yvette decided she would apply for the position. Within a couple of weeks, she was hired. Not long after,

I went to work in the warehouse of a local company working second shift. I didn't like the job, nor did I care for the hours. But at least we both were working. With money now coming in, we were able to move into a one-bedroom apartment.

While Yvette was enjoying her job, and the surroundings, she was unaware of the challenges I was facing at work, the biggest of which was having to resist the temptation when some of my coworkers would ask me to go out drinking with them after work. They knew nothing of my past, and I wasn't about to tell them. Thankfully, each time I was asked to go out I had strength to say no.

Yvette started encouraging me to apply for work at KCM so we could be together. Each time, I refused because I didn't want to work for a ministry. She continued to urge me to apply, and eventually I gave in.

Little did I know that I was walking straight into God's plan for my life.

Not long after we'd move into an apartment, and our finances were stable, Yvette and I started looking to buy a house. We found one we liked, contacted a realtor, and made an offer. Then, the unthinkable happened—I was fired from my warehouse job. It seems I was not compatible with those I worked with.

I'll never forget the day that happened, or how I reacted when I called Yvette to give her the news.

"I got fired," I told her.

Then, I started laughing.

Why? I don't really know. What I do know, though, is that I was relieved. And I felt a certain peace.

Yvette, on the other hand, didn't think my being fired was funny at all.

"What about the house we just made an offer on," she asked.

"Call the realtor and let them know," I told her.

Instead, Yvette prayed and asked God to help.

A few days later, I received a call from KCM offering me a job working in the ministry's warehouse. Within a few weeks, we closed on our new home.

The environment at KCM was electric. Everywhere you went on the property, you were surrounded by God's Word. In some ways, it reminded me of my experience when I would go to my aunt's church back in Juárez. The more I listened to the teachings by Kenneth and Gloria Copeland, as well as some ministers who would often visit the ministry, the more I learned about God. Suddenly, what I had heard those many years ago, that God loved me, began to make sense.

Then, one day while listening to a message by Kenneth Copeland I heard him say something that caught my attention.

"You are the prophet of your own life!"

Me, the prophet of my own life? I wondered. What exactly does that mean?

I found the answer when I decided to pursue more of Brother Copeland's teaching on the subject. In one article I read by Brother Copeland, he explained it this way:

> "You are the prophet of your own life."

"People have always had the idea that prophets are "special. The truth, however, is that anyone called by God—prophet or not— is no different than the rest of us. Prophets are just people—not "special" people. What makes them different is the anointing, the power that God gives them to do 'special' things... You and I are anointed to confess our sins and be forgiven. We're anointed to confess God's Word and be healed. We're anointed to confess

God's Word and live in health. We're anointed to confess God's Word and live in wealth. We're anointed to confess God's Word and prosper in our souls. We are anointed to speak the Word and prosper in every way! We are the prophets of our own lives... Your future—good or bad—is in you, right now. It's in your mouth and it's determined by the words you speak... Simply put, you and I are what we are today—and we have what we have today—because of what we said yesterday."

Suddenly, I got it. In a nutshell, life is about the choices we make. That revelation set me on a course that would eventually change my life forever. I would soon learn that my being at KCM was not by chance, nor accident. God was about to open doors for me to share my story with hundreds of people around the world and see the lives of many changed.

In 2006, not long after I started working for the ministry, I was approached and asked to travel to Venezuela with the KCM ministry team. The person who served as translator for Brother Copeland was not able to make the trip, and they wanted me to fill in for him. Holding a microphone for the first time in my life, I ministered the Word of God in Spanish as Brother Copeland preached.

It was an experience I will never forget, primarily because I saw God work a miracle for me, and the ministry.

It was a Saturday, and I had flown to Maracaibo, Venezuela, South America as part of the advance team. Brother Copeland, who was scheduled to minister there the following Friday, was to fly out from Fort Worth the following Thursday and arrived in Maracaibo around noon. On Wednesday, the day before Brother Copeland was to leave Fort Worth, we were notified that we still had not received the proper permissions from the city for Brother Copeland's airplane to land there. This was despite the fact that the ministry had filled out and submitted all the paperwork required to obtain permits. The ministry had already leased the venue where the meeting was to be held, and advertisement for the meeting had been circulating for months.

On Wednesday, the day before Brother Copeland was scheduled to fly to Venezuela, we still did not have the proper permits. After making several appeals to officials, it was suggested that, due to the urgency, we speak directly with someone in the office of civil aviation, which is located in Caracas. Surprisingly, I was asked to be spokesman. Someone else from our team travelled with me.

Caracas is a 12-hour drive by car, but only one hour by air. The ticket counter at the airport closed at 6 o'clock, giving us only 30-minutes to get there. We flew out at 6 a.m. on Thursday. The civil aviation office opened at 8 a.m.

Because our paperwork had already been submitted, I didn't think getting the permits would be a problem. Upon explaining our dilemma to the desk clerk, we were told the Minister of Civil Aviation would not be available to speak with us until the following Tuesday. After further expressing the importance of getting the permits, and that Brother Copeland was scheduled to fly out at noon that day, I gave her one of the flyers promoting the meeting and asked if she would at least show it to her boss.

She agreed.

Meanwhile, I went off to pray and asked God for favor.

About 30 minutes later, I was sitting in a reception area filled with people when a voice said: "Senor Sergio Alvarado, the minister will see you know." At the moment, no words had ever sounded so good.

As I walked into the office, I was greeted by a very distinguished-looking gentleman. In his hand, he held the flyer I had given to the receptionist.

He spoke to me in Spanish, saying "Que dios te bendiga," which means "God bless you."

His next words shocked me.

"So, you work with Brother Copeland," he asked.

"Yes sir," I answered. "Do you know him?"

"I have been watching him for years on TV, and he has made an impact on my life and my family's life. So, what can I do for you?"

After explaining our situation, the minister called his secretary in and asked her to bring him our paperwork. Within 15 minutes, we had the permits we needed.

We thanked the minister, and then we prayed together.

One hour before Brother Copeland was scheduled to fly out to Venezuela, we had the permits we needed. The meeting went off without a hitch and was very successful.

If I didn't know where my life was headed before, that single incident caused me to see that God truly had a plan to use me. All I needed to do was listen for His voice and obey whatever He told me to do. That, I believe, was a big part of what Brother Copeland meant when he spoke those words, "You are the prophet of your own life!"

Now part of KCM's ministry team, I travel to meetings across the country. In one of those meetings, Brother Copeland invited me to the platform to share my testimony. Before an audience of thousands, I listened humbly as he said to the audience, "I want to introduce you to my spiritual son."

> God had restored to me what had been lost.

My mother had rejected me. My father had abandoned me. Yet this man of God called me his son.

God had restored to me what had been lost.

A Lifeline to the Hurting

In March 2014, I returned to Juárez with a burden in my heart for the people.

Once again, I stood in the basketball stadium where, as a child, I had sold potato chips and where my mother worked the bar and sold her body. Only this time, at the Lord's direction, I had rented the stadium and was about to host the first ever Juárez Victory Campaign. Instead of a sporting event, the stands were filled with people praising the Name of Jesus.

The crowd watched a stirring message by Brother Copeland on video.

I had returned to Juárez because God had given me a new direction.

The city is still considered one of the most dangerous cities on earth. Many of its children are still trapped in a vicious cycle surrounded by drugs with no way out. God has called me to help—to throw out a lifeline so they can know there is hope. One of the ways God is helping me do that is by building a church in Juárez—a place where young children can find hope through God's Word.

Currently, I am in the process of purchasing land in the same area where I lived. Through our ministry, we are raising funds to construct a church, equipped with a large kitchen where the children can be fed and nourished.

God has called me to throw out a lifeline to hurting people around the world, but specifically to the children living in Juárez—to reverse the curse in their lives, just as He did for me. I was a product of my environment, and there was no one there to help pull me out. Today, I know what it means to be the prophet of my own life. I know the value of God's Word and the importance of speaking it. I know that God is truly on my side.

As I reflect on my past, and all the Lord has done to set me free from it, and put me on the right path so that He can fulfill His plan and purpose in my life, I constantly remind myself of His Word in Deuteronomy

30:19, New Living Translation, which says, "Today I have given you the choice between life and death, between blessings and curses. Now I call on heaven and earth to witness the choice you make. Oh, that you would choose life, so that you and your descendants might live!" In life, we all have choices. When we make bad choices, we open ourselves to the possibility of bad things happening to us.

The Bible tells us in James 4:7, "Submit therefore to God. Resist the devil and he will flee from you. That's God's formula for survival—it's His blueprint for avoiding the traps and pitfalls the devil has laid out for us and positioning ourselves to live the blessed, prosperous and productive life He has for us.

Seventeen years ago, I grabbed a lifeline from God that turned my life around. His Word gave me new life. It gave me hope and victory. And today, I want to throw out that same lifeline to others. Perhaps you are one of those. If so, I want you to know that whatever it is you're going through, whatever the devil is using to try to hold you back, there is hope. If you will resist his deceptive attempts, be courageous and submit your life to the only One who can save you, God will help you survive. He will help you to become the prophet of your own life!

Prayer for Salvation and Baptism in the Holy Spirit

Heavenly Father, I come to You in the Name of Jesus. Your Word says, "Whosoever shall call on the name of the Lord shall be saved" (Acts 2:21). I am calling on You. I pray and ask Jesus to come into my heart and be Lord over my life according to Romans 10:9-10: "If thou shalt confess with thy mouth the Lord Jesus, and shalt believe in thine heart that God hath raised him from the dead, thou shalt be saved. For with the heart man believeth unto righteousness; and with the mouth confession is made unto salvation." I do that now. I confess that Jesus is Lord, and I believe in my heart that God raised Him from the dead.

I am now reborn! I am a Christian—a child of Almighty God! I am saved! You also said in Your Word, "If ye then, being evil, know how to give good gifts unto your children: HOW MUCH MORE shall your heavenly Father give the Holy Spirit to them that ask him?" (Luke 11:13). I'm also asking You to fill me with the Holy Spirit. Holy

Spirit, rise up within me as I praise God. I fully expect to speak with other tongues as You give me the utterance (Acts 2:4). In Jesus' Name. Amen!

Begin to praise God for filling you with the Holy Spirit. Speak those words and syllables you receive—not in your own language, but the language given to you by the Holy Spirit. You have to use your own voice. God will not force you to speak. Don't be concerned with how it sounds. It is a heavenly language!

Continue with the blessing God has given you and pray in the spirit every day.

You are a born-again, Spirit-filled believer. You'll never be the same!

Find a good church that boldly preaches God's Word and obeys it. Become part of a church family who will love and care for you as you love and care for them.

We need to be connected to each other. It increases our strength in God. It's God's plan for us.

If you would like to sow into the lives of children in Juárez:

Visit:

www.alvaradoministriesinternational.org

Write to:

Sergio Alvarado
Alvarado Ministries International
PO Box 1548
Springtown, TX 76082

(Your contributions are tax deductible.)

CPSIA information can be obtained
at www.ICGtesting.com
Printed in the USA
FSHW010250181119